I0846195

By Jenni L Medina

For my loving wife, Kristina Medina, and our families.

WHAT A REVEALING SECRET (not really)

What is a challenge? Perhaps, it's a round of pool at your cousin's house, an eating contest, or a spelling bee. These are challenges faced by average people just like you or me. I think we all know the more difficult challenges in life; rent is due, putting food on the table, running water, kids need to eat, juggling schoolwork plus actual job work, and a busy life, the death of a loved one, etc. What does all of it even mean? Is it a circle of tasks to keep us busy till our final day? Is there a bigger picture we aren't able to see? What about the successful people and friends you went to school with that are doing "big" things with their lives, or are in happy relationships? Do we commend them for doing the very things we always planned to but never quite made it as far as them, yet? Wouldn't we want to be admired or praised or congratulated when we accomplish the things we always wanted to? Bet you that things didn't go your way thus far. Here's a little secret; unless someone in life has an indescribable amount of discipline and will-power, things hardly go the way anyone wants it to. Life happens. Behind every success story is one of two things; someone who never had anything handed to them and understood the value of their hard work and nothing short of, or the person that has had privilege dropped into their lap and opportunity served to them on a silver platter. It's not our place to judge. All we can do is be happy for the ones that made it. The cop, the doctor, the music therapist, the lawyer, the actor, the backup dancer. Our happiness for others essentially tells us more about ourselves than our own success. You can be the most successful individual of your lifetime, and still be referred to as a martyr, a Debby downer, a shitbag.

      Start with you. Take a cold hard look at the person you are. My guess is you haven't in quite some time. After all, you're busy! Don't ask 'how did I end up here,' but ask yourself 'what can I improve in order to move up in my life or be just a little happier?' Baby steps. Appreciate what you do have, for one. That's for starters. I bet you didn't know anxiety was a healthy emotion. I bet you didn't know fear was natural, even in the silliest of situations. Have you ever been so scared or so unbelievably sad you wanted to die? Or felt as if you were dying? This is all relatively normal. 1 in 4 people in the world suffer from a mental disorder. They can be quite challenging and hold us back from accomplishing our dreams. How can we overcome these things and finally put forth the first step into the next chapter of our lives? Although there are steps to it, there's also a need for constancy.

      There's a very large gap between emotional depression and schizophrenia. With hallucinations, visions, voices being heard that aren't there, and paranoia that causes you to run and hide in a corner, this most definitely will require medication or some sort of external management. If you have anxiety and depression, did you know that you can be your own doctor? Not only to manage these things, but to make a big part of it go away.

      Maybe not for good, but at least go away to the point that it becomes an acquaintance in bypassing rather than a toxic best friend. Remember that co-worker that you don't really know well and gives you a bad impression but then over time you guys understand each other, and now there's peace and harmony in the workplace? Depression and anxiety, once understood, become your strengths. As corny as it may sounds, the cure is in you. The cure is also in the Earth. Now, don't start imagining peace pipes and essential oils and natural CBD. When I say the Earth, I'm referring to our essential elements, not oils. Water, light, air. Every beautiful plant-life requires photosynthesis to happen. We learn this in science class in elementary school…well guess what, we need photosynthesis too (in a way). We are basically an unstable bunch of trees or flowers, if you will. Too much intelligence can kill you. Our brains can make or break our lives. We say our hearts are essential to live, but without the feel of purpose, without even the slightest bit of paranoia, our hearts don't beat quite the same. You're not abnormal for feeling how you do. We're all different, and quite on purpose.

In times of my depression and stress, my go-to was either to lay on the couch in fear of leaving the house, or food, in fear of social interaction. Either way, it wasn't healthy. I chose to go to a doctor to get checked…never a bad thing. The doctor was free (temporarily) for me because I didn't have health insurance, but after a few free sessions and prescribed medication (antidepressant) I was out of sessions. I was depressed and anxious to a degree in which it debilitated me physically and mentally from being able to hold a job or sleep right, if at all. I once lied awake for 72 hours and thought I was going to die. The exhaustion was unlike anything I had ever felt. I was never one to smoke or drink, so I chose to just deal with it. I had no other way of managing it besides this medication. The doctor never instructed me on how to withdraw from it in a healthy way. I was written a script and sent on my way. I had a year supply of Celexa and was supposed to be weaning myself off at 6 months. Of course, I didn't find this out till much later. By then, it was too late. I was hooked. I went to the emergency room time and time again for extreme panic attacks, trying to get some type of medication to calm my nerves and help me sleep.

I thought other things were wrong with me, but the results were always normal. I was afraid of my own mind. My thoughts carried me to a place of fear. Never in my life did I feel only one emotion take over at once known as fear. That fear carried me into another year of being addicted to antidepressants and straight into a toxic relationship, that I one day convinced myself I needed, and eventually chose to marry this person. My self-worth depleted.

Over the course of 5 years I became much better at handling things and got myself off the medication and up off the couch, once and for all. How? Someone once told me, "I know you don't feel like doing this, but you never will feel like it. You have to just force yourself. Get up and walk." So, I walked. I soaked in the Sun; I looked at my surroundings. I went down a different path every day. It was a bit scary at first. Sometimes I drove myself to a different area, wide open with a body of water, whether it was a beach or a lake, and I walked. Walking became a habit. Leaving my surroundings also became the very thing I needed to remove myself, metaphorically, from the dark places in my head. No, your problems do not go away the second you leave the area. Your Earthly problems will always follow you, but your mental problems can be metaphorically dismissed or resumed, depending on your choices. I chose to leave my hometown because that is where I felt "in the dark." My mental state was in a hospice state. Every day I thought it was over for me. I thought 'this is the day that my mind will cease me.' I was wrong. Our minds are much stronger than we think. Any time I went to a new place or traveled to a new state, or taken a walk down an unfamiliar path, I felt better and better each time. The toxic relationship I was in was the only thing weighing heavy on me. It was something that I let get the best of me. I was abused mentally, physically and emotionally. It was hard to leave the area, because all I wanted to do was stay where the person I loved most, was. She was never leaving anytime soon. I was stuck. I knew I was in a terrible situation, but I felt bound. I kept justifying her behavior and everything happening, blaming it on her own mental illness, and just dealt with things as they were. I never thought to myself, not once, that things could be better. I figured, they would get better with this person and with time.

I settled. I hadn't thought much of myself, and I hadn't looked at myself in the mirror in years, so why would I ever think I deserve someone better than a person that deliberately wanted to hurt me? It was a mystery then, but not so much now. You accept being treated just as the person you think of yourself as. Regardless of the situation, when someone brings you to your lowest point, that person should not be in your life; family, friends, etc. Doesn't matter. Walking. That was my baby step.

Pretty soon I was able to eat some food and keep it down, thanks to my cousins Heather and Ben. Rice and a bottle of Ensure. That was my other baby step. I couldn't figure out why I was this down, and when I did my own research, I self-diagnosed myself with a simple chemical imbalance. Simple diagnosis but not so simple to deal with. That's all anxiety and depression really is. Some choose to use outside management. Others choose to internally build themselves back up again. I wasn't sure what I was able to do. I didn't believe in myself. I felt no one believed in me, either. All they would say to me is to "get a job" or "let her go." All of it much easier said than done. Just as effective as telling a drug addict to "put down the needle and don't do it anymore." It's not that simple. If it was, no one would smoke a damn thing or need a beer after work. If you've ever had a panic attack, you know what it feels like. It seems like you can't breathe, and death is coming for you. A panic attack, scientifically, is essentially your body intaking too much oxygen. Go figure. Of course, there's a little more to it, but I'm not a doctor.

Knowing these things helped me eventually deal with all of the panic attacks and chemical imbalances. Not at first, but eventually. I was told to hold my breath for five seconds and let it out slowly about ten times; this worked for me but doesn't always work for others.

A SECOND CHAPTER

When's the last time you had a sense of accomplishment? Whether it was you finishing school, getting a promotion at work, buying a home, or sticking to a diet/gym plan? You get the idea. When I joined the Army, I was finally at my low point. I reached a point in time when I didn't care what happened to me. I started to care only of what happened to others. I thought to myself, what is the one thing I can leave behind that fulfills me with a sense of purpose? I had lost all purpose within me. At first, I looked into The Peace Corp. Turns out they require you to have a Humanities degree, and I had nothing. I talked to a prior Marine a while after, and eventually sought out a recruiter for the Army; their job is to ultimately sell you on the lifestyle of a soldier. They fill you in on how you'll go to all these military schools and once you become full-time Army, they'll pay for college and your living expenses, your food, free health care, the whole shebang. By then, I was turning 26, and already had fallen so many times in life. The girl I had always put my life on hold for, broke up with me the day I enlisted. She and I had always been back and forth, but the breaks would never last longer than a week. I was shipping off in a month for Basic Training. This was it. This was goodbye for good.

The one thing that can cure depression and anxiety is distraction. An extreme distraction; a healthy distraction, that is. A total life-change. I threw myself whole-heartedly into a life I didn't know for sure that I wanted, but I knew I needed to change. I was tired of the person I was and tired of being tired. The funny thing about extreme distraction is when you are distracted, you begin to get reacquainted with who you are when you least expect it. That's what I had to do. That's what everyone who feels lost has to do. When you were a child, you knew yourself frontwards and backwards. There was no questioning whether or not you liked macaroni and cheese or hated brussels sprouts. The second someone put one of those things in front of you, you knew which one you were going to go for. The same thing happens as an adult except now, our choices are being made with much more thought behind it. It's not a bad thing to try new food, but when you ultimately know what works or doesn't work for you, there's no sense in second guessing yourself. That's something we as adults do too much of.

In Basic Training, I had no time to second guess myself. There were times I was told to run and jump over a log that was level to my height or run into a building and "save" a soldier by carrying them out of a building during open fire. I was also told to crawl in pitch black under barbed wire while bombs and flares went off above me. The simulation of a battlefield really taught me something. I needed to be following my instincts, even if it was the hardest thing to do. I made it to the other side of the field in pitch black, unharmed and ready to go. We know when something isn't working, or something isn't good for us. We know when we could be doing better. So why don't we do it? Simple. We think we don't know what's good for us because we don't know ourselves anymore.

Somewhere along the lines, we flew off the hinges and went down different paths only to come to a fork in the road. At that point, we tossed a coin and gambled on our next decision. Also, your mind is your very own atmosphere. Sometimes, it rains. Sometimes, it's just cloudy with light thunderstorms. Unlike a quarterly change in weather, the weather can be different every day. One day it can snow and the very next be a blue-sky Summer day. Getting a hold of our own minds means we become the meteorologist. We can now predict when the rain is going to come and when the sunny skies will brighten up our days. We are in control. Once in a blue moon, you'll experience an Earthquake; an unpredictable disturbance in our minds that shatters our walls and fills our minds with debris. These are things like, deaths In the family, finding out our spouse is cheating, or you're pregnant. Our lives are suddenly turned upside down. What do we do at this point? It's up to us to know how to handle our emotions. Some of us choose weed, alcohol, opioids, to go back to an ex, rage, food, isolation. Each one ranks a certain level of danger to our mental stability, simply due to the fact that now, it's a dependency. We no longer trust ourselves, so now we trust other things more. We can certainly be addicted to being isolated, though some people don't think so. The biggest cause of isolation is a toxic relationship. The need for one's approval and the inability to attain it. Logically, if a child does something bad and knows what they're doing is bad, they're not going to flaunt it or share it with the people they're most afraid of disappointing. When the relationship is toxic and we know it, we hide in order to avoid judgment. Isolation is also an addiction caused by depression itself. When someone is depressed, they can feel embarrassed by it. They feel weak and unable to handle the extremity of their emotions. I, too, once felt this way. My family has yet to know just how many times I ended up in the emergency room for a panic attack. It isn't fair that we feel so desperate to blend into the world around us that when we're even the slightest bit different or inconvenient in any way, we shut down or put on a front.

A STEPPING STONE

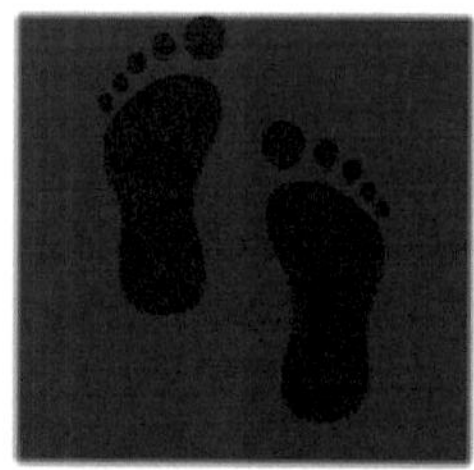

The rates of suicide are at an all-time high these days. This world becomes harder to live in each day people are shamed for feeling a certain way or making certain mistakes. Luckily, there is a way out; a light at the end of a tunnel that we can't see, yet. When you're in a dark place it's hard to see any light switches. Remember how I said to walk? The more you walk, the closer you'll get. When you're at your lowest, there's only one other way to go. Key number one: Find yourself. Key number two: Get reacquainted with the person you originally were before all the things that dimmed your light. Key number three: Make yourself a priority. Key number four: Rise above the shame and guilt. Key number five: Maintain your mental health above all things.

Occasionally, I struggle with anxiety and panic attacks. Mostly its due to large crowds. Rarely does this happen, but when it does, CBD gummies work for me. Most of the time, I try to deal with it myself. I mentally challenge myself each day to think my way back to home plate. When your thoughts run away with you, it's easy to feel scared and like you can never turn back around. This isn't true. Follow your positive instincts, always. When they're difficult to find, take a walk. There's plenty of actions you can take to jog your thoughts and bring your mental state back to a full-blown balance; one you'll become well-adjusted to. These steps are literal steps I've taken. Nothing beyond this point is metaphorical, and none of it is easy, but once you do it, they become your natural way of handling things. No more dependency on anything or anyone. Just you.

WHAT WORKS (the 7+)

Step 1: WALK. Occasionally, jog. Do what the Army calls 30-60's. Run for 30 seconds then walk for 60 seconds. Do this over the course of 20 minutes or as long as you feel necessary, making sure your scenery is pleasant, or different than the day before. Experiencing different sensations and views rewires our brain to intake more information rather than turning to what's familiar. What's familiar to us may be toxic, so getting out of the habit of turning to familiarity, is step number one. While walking or jogging, listen to happy music. Listen to music that brings our souls alive and tears of joy to our eyes. Listen to motivational speakers, childhood music, movie soundtracks, and nothing mundane, sad or angry. Leave that at home. You may even find it calming to listen to your natural surroundings.

Step 2: Eat! It doesn't matter if you're hungry or not during depression and anxiety. When we're depressed/anxious, some turn to food, but others do not. Always eat anyway. Even if it's just a little. If you turn to food for comfort, eat a better meal. Cheese and eggs, or fruit, oatmeal, peanut butter and jelly sandwiches, something not

so sugary or frozen. Turning to decent or extremely healthy food and just filling our stomach up whether we like it or not, will force our bodies into a healthier state. Right now, your body is a reflection of your mind. If you're stressed, your body responds poorly. We don't usually listen to our bodies when it tells us something. We turn to bed and a TV or a nightclub. Our bodies need stimulation. Think of it as your body and mind were best friends growing up but had a falling-out. Now, they need to get reacquainted. Fuel it with something satisfying and healthy. Set alarms on your phone every few hours to eat a snack or fruit. Almonds, apples, anything, because even if you're not hungry, your body needs things that your mind just will not give into just yet. A healthy meal also assists in the brain chemical department with rebalancing everything out. Your body and mind need to work together!

Step 3: Be by yourself. That's not to say isolate yourself. Set aside time for you and spend it wisely. If you have a family, tend to them. Doing what we need to for others, whether it's our children or our spouse or siblings, allows us to still be a shoulder to lean on as we battle our own dark thoughts. Don't lose this. Also, whether you have a family or not, spend time alone. Not just in your room or on the couch alone; in public! That's right. There's a big difference in being out and about and being alone in your room. Integrate yourself in society. Go to the movies, go skating, go to the zoo (do day-time activities that don't require you to drink/smoke, and lose the phone!) you can go to a community pool, a dog shelter to walk around, stores, a mall in particular. Try not to use your phone or look at social media. Do this at least twice a week for perhaps an hour; longer if you can make it. Take yourself out to eat also. Alone!

Take yourself on dates. Here's why. We do not value our time or ourselves as much as we should. We feel like our time is best spent with others or working and in our alone time, we choose to go to what's familiar; our bed and some Netflix. That's perfectly fine for a chill day after a long week, but in this process of trying to rebuild our minds and emotional stability, we need to refrain from this mindset for now. If you choose to do anything like go hiking or to the ocean, let someone know where you are as a safety precaution, not as an invite. Go to a comedy show, a magic show. Do all these things for the next few months.

Take one or two days out of the week and make sure you do something for YOU. You can also get crazy and go to an amusement park. You may be called "lame" in terms of it being abnormal to experience these things alone, but you need to find yourself again. That kid that grew up feeling and thinking outside the box, running carefree and talking to whomever talked back, senseless laughter, and just overall happiness, is still in you. When you find them, you'll never let them go. All activities in your life will have that soulful being shine through and you'll finally be able to enjoy being in the moment. You'll finally appreciate your family, your good friends and your kids. This one is the hardest step because rarely can someone pull this off. They see it as a challenge. Accept the challenge! You won't regret it. Going to the park to read or feed the ducks or any day-time activity we do alone is actually necessary in order for us to recover from anxiety/depression. Talk to yourself and talk yourself through your thoughts and be clear about your emotions before the next step.

Step 4: Talk! Not only should you talk to yourself in the car or in the house alone when you're trying to figure out conflicting points of views or a conflict in general, but also

talking to friends and family is an enormous plus when trying to recuperate from an extreme depression or immense anxiety. Talking out loud allows us to verbally sort through things and gain perspective before handling anything.

Talking to others allows us to feel the sensation of togetherness and steer us away from feeling entirely alone. It's one thing to try and be okay with being by ourselves and alone with our thoughts, and another to bask in a depression alone. We want to make sure that when we're by ourselves we're still doing what's best for us, and when we're with others, we're with someone we can trust and confide in with an absence of judgment. Let someone know you're down. Especially, if it applies, let someone know if you ever feel like harming yourself or if you feel like death is the only option for you. I've been there. Death is scary, but to some people it represents peace.

This life is exciting. It's full of heartache and pain but equally full of color and an unimaginable amount of happiness if we just give it a chance. All of this will take time, but right off the bat, you should feel a difference just from step 3. This is the step, as I mentioned before, people forget to do, but is the most important. Don't skip it! Talking is sometimes an uncomfortable thing for people to do. Some want to only talk to a select number of people, some only choose to do it in therapy, and others hate talking altogether and refuse to talk through their pain. This is part of the 'letting go of what's familiar,' thing. Try this new level of speaking. Talk to a random friend you hadn't in a long time. Talk to family that you're most comfortable with. If you're in the park and someone else is alone, strike up a casual conversation without getting personal. A random conversation about anything and everything is mentally stimulating and is essential in this step as well. Don't only talk about your issues. Talk about life, talk about your past, talk about things you haven't dealt with yet. Make jokes. Whatever you feel is most suited for the circumstances you're in, is exactly how you should proceed.

Step 5: Attain a sense of accomplishment. Baby steps, once more. The Army provided me with a sense of accomplishment because I was doing things I never thought I'd do in my life that improved my mental stamina, and physical fitness. You don't need the Army, or college, though these things provide enormous amounts of the accomplishment factor. Attain small goals and set long term goals for yourself. Take up boxing and get to new levels. Take on Tae Kwon Do and attain new belts. Take dance courses and get amazing at it. Take up surfing lessons, motorcycle lessons, biking, weight goals, join a support group, etc. New things you've never done before and

wish to accomplish are small and reasonable goals you can achieve that fulfill this step. Take up a certificate program (generally a year or less) so you're able to graduate and become an expert in that particular field, whether it's for shits and gigs, or for the long hall. A job you've always wanted. One accomplishment that isn't always thought of as one, but surely is, is to make amends. Those that you've done wrong in the past or have had a falling-out with over time, or if you've done someone wrong, make amends. It helps to lift the burdens that secretly weight us down.

Also, during this time, do NOT under any circumstances, compare yourself to others and their timeline. This is your life, not theirs. There are many people out there as it is, wishing they were you or at your stage in life even if you don't feel you're far along enough. You're exactly where you should be. Remember, from this point on, there's nowhere to go but up. Even if your goals are as small as, how far you choose to walk versus how far you walked the day before, it's a small step for your body, but a giant step for your mental growth.

Step 6: Join the people you love during events or outings, specifically, not just a casual hangout. Avoid isolation. The worst feeling is being in a crowd yet feeling alone. I'm confident that when you discover yourself, your likes your dislikes, your passions, and feel that self-worth flood your mind, body and soul, you'll no longer feel the need to be a crowd pleaser. You'll no longer resort to becoming a Debby downer or feel the need to leave an event early so you can

be alone with your thoughts and feelings. You'll for once be able to channel everything in a healthy way, so you can function in this world to the best of your ability. Success won't always manifest itself nor come in the form of a college degree or wealth.

Success will come to you when that sense of accomplishment is so satisfying that you're ready to move onto the next accomplishment, and the next one after that. Let those around you, big circle of support or small or none, be a part of your success.

Step 7: It's easy to go backwards in life. So easy in fact, if I wanted to at this very moment, I can quit working, quit school, and live out of my car that they'll eventually repo. So simple. It's easy to give up, but not easy to maintain happiness at the same time. If we want this happiness to last, we must continue up the steep hill of issues, battle through the depths of our emotions, and conquer it all. Occasionally, I let myself slip back into a mental state of doubt and worry. When my life went from great to horrible, to mediocre then horrific, to stable then unstable, so on and so forth, the fluctuation of my health, hormones and mental stability was almost too much to handle. It's in those rare moments during recovery, that we must remember these steps. If my mind begins to slip, I open the door to the outside. On rainy days, I slipped into a movie theater to watch a comedy. These are the moments we remember just how human we really are, and we remember where we've been. Over the course of a year or two, it becomes much harder for our minds to slip backwards after putting forth the effort every single day that is required for us, individually. Our bodies and our minds have become so used to handling the anxiety and depression and unexpected panic attacks so much, that we almost forget what it feels

like. All we know is we never want to feel it again. Speaking of panic attacks...

Special step: This is for those that experience panic attacks. I'm not going to lie, I get them on occasion; as I mentioned previously, large crowds are what do it for me. I begin to feel dizzy, the tingling sensations run all up and down my face and I begin to tremble. Breathing becomes shallow. Sometimes I just want to run the other way. Sometimes it's necessary to do so, as long as you're safe. Other times, I try to sit there and think the panic attack away, which rarely works at all. It's an embarrassing moment to have to stand up from a random hangout with friends or a concert you've always wanted to go to, and just walk away...no explanation, no warning. Everyone's trigger for panic attacks are different. As I said before, I use CBD gummies, because in those moments, there's nothing else that will calm me. I've tried many things without turning to substances. Nothing else works. Mind you, this happens to me about twice a month at the most, fortunately. For others, they're not so fortunate. Some people can experience this awful sensation weekly or daily. I commend you for making it through those difficult times, because it's one of the hardest things to overcome. Maybe most of you have heard this before, but for those of you that haven't, I'll say what also helps besides CBD supplements; name three things you can see...then name three things you can smell...three things you can taste...three things you can touch...three things you can hear. In the moment, this may be hard to remember. Explain to the person you spend the most time with, how this works. Inform them that these are the ways to help you regain your grip of reality and help calm you down. Make sure this is someone you trust. Also, take a deep breath (as deep as you can) and hold it for five seconds. Let the air out slowly. This calms the heart rate and allows you to act on the other helpful tips more effectively.

If we're physically feeling out of control, it's difficult to smell, taste, hear, see or feel anything at all. When a panic attack hits, take a walk, but never alone. If you're alone, call someone immediately. If you cannot call someone, remember these helpful guidelines, and find a fast-working supplement that is natural and works for these moments and these moments only. This should not be your "go-to," but if nothing else works, use it. I don't condone weed or drugs or anything of the sort, but edibles that contain CBD and are CO2 extracted are beneficial in times like this and cannot harm us or cloud our judgment.

This is important if you're planning on regaining emotional strength. In saying all this, panic attacks are downright scary. They can only be explained through the eyes of those that have experienced them. Being told to "try to calm down" or "don't panic" is a silly statement and should never be used when trying to calm someone that's in a state of panic. This is strictly a reaction of a chemical/oxygen imbalance and has nothing to do with worry or fear. Fear of death and worry just happen to be the symptoms. My wife and I are very different when it comes to this. CBD does not work for her. She needs a stronger supplement of the same sort. I, on the other hand, am a lightweight when it comes to anything, especially medication. The CBD gummies work wonders on me and allow me to sleep at night. It's both healthy and has zero side effects.

This is my wife, Kristina. She's an accomplished woman in various areas of life and happens to be an Army Veteran as well. Sometimes depression looks happy, as I'm sure some of you know this. Many have a tendency to be social butterflies yet hold every burden they've ever had, inside. It weighs heavy. That's Kristina. She overworks herself into the ground when she feels the most stress. Although it's healthy to work and attain that sense of accomplishment as I spoke about, finding balance is also important. If you have a family, kids, a home to take care of, you're not good to them if you're held up at work 9/10ths of the time. We decided to seek marriage counseling out of the pure need to be closer. Others hear this and think "oh, they must have problems!" Quite the contrary! We do things as a couple and seek therapy so that our marriage remains intact during any hardship. We already work as a team so wonderfully and are best-friends underneath it all.

At the end of the day, I don't only get to go home to my wife, but I get to vent to my best friend and she's always helped me through. I do the same for her. Therapy is almost a necessity for anyone wanting a successful marriage and family unit, especially if you have a blended family. Without therapy, and with all the busy schedules in the home, it's hard to find that time to bond and reconnect. Because of this, we constantly date, we are in constant communication, and we've never been happier with each other. That's not to say there isn't bad days and we don't each have our flaws, but we understand each other to an extent most young couples do not. Understanding each other is key!

Kristina tends to want job on top of job, and although on paper this looks fantastic, her constant need for

distraction is also a negative coping mechanism. Her and I are very different when it comes to dealing with our emotions. I wear my heart on my sleeve and make sure to make some noise on the subject at hand. As for Kristina, you wouldn't know what's bothering her until one day she snaps about spilling water on the floor. Water doesn't stain, and we have wooden floors and tile. Not a big deal. To her, it's a huge deal, because last week when she didn't get the raise she was promised (hypothetically speaking), she saw it as a failure and since work had consumed her so greatly, it was everything to her. Her accomplishments and let downs were all within that one job. That is why I stress the importance of balance. If you were to put all your heart and soul into a toxic relationship, that toxic relationship becomes your sense of accomplishment and failure as well. It's important that, if you have kids, to make your child(ren) a priority as a sense of accomplishment of yours. It's also important to strive for greatness when it comes to school, work, assisting your grandparents, being a good friend to someone. Why? Because without this balance, you are your relationship, and that's it. You are their wife, girlfriend, and that's it. You are an employee/manager, and that's it; that is the extent of your life. This cannot be, especially when dealing with depression and anxiety. They do not discriminate. This is why we see celebrities so down and depressed a lot of the time because their heart and soul has been poured into showbiz, and they have no other sense of self-worth. Find your worth.

I once asked Kristina, "Why do you like working so much?" She says, "I love working because I like to be in charge of something." I asked her another time, "Hey, why do you feel like you have to be working all the time? Our money is good without it!" She says, "We need more money after this last month." In the beginning of our relationship, when I first asked her why she has a second job while still active duty military, she said, "I can't sleep, so if I'm tired out, it helps me." She also said, "My ex-wife refused to work, so I needed to make up the income." All of these answers were true and still are true; however, the answers constantly changed. I began to wonder why and then it dawned on me. This is her "go-to." Whenever things are out of whack, the one thing that is structured and dignified and also a great disguise for someone who's down in the dumps, is a job.

My wife has chronic back pain and has had spine surgery. The last thing she should ever be doing is over working herself, not just physically, but mentally, since we carry all of our stress in our backs and shoulders. Does she ever take my advice? No, but she does compromise. She agrees to have certain days off specifically so we can be together and also perhaps taking care of the house, lounge around, run errands, whichever is needed at the time. I want those to see that there is no right or wrong nor only one way to express depression and anxiety. Kristina cries out of anger or frustration, not because she's sad. This is a common reaction, however, revealing. All defense is gone at her most pressing times. Everyone is testing her limits, and finally, the walls come down and all the problems over the years pour out in just one cry. The issue with this is, it can happen at the wrong time. You may accidentally take out your anger on someone who has nothing to do with your anger, or act out in a way you normally wouldn't, such as calling off work. We all need mental health days away from work and away from mundane activities, but regulating our emotions and keeping this balance, will retrain our brains to not let our emotions interfere with our lives.

Now that I've clarified for you the many ways to handle anxiety and depression, I'll leave you with this:

IN CONCLUSION

The reason I do not condone drugs or weed or smoking/drinking of any sort in order to deal with emotional needs, is because our minds are strong and delicate all at the same time. If you're younger than 26 years of age, your mind is still developing, and the second you pick up anything that alters your mind/emotions/judgment and make it a habit, your brain's emotional development momentum comes to a screeching halt. Should that very thing disappear one day, your baggage will be right there waiting for you. Anger comes on easier and stronger, emotions weigh more than they should, and depression is more prone to hit, when it could've been avoided altogether. Not to mention it's a big money saver to not rely on anything but ourselves and the loved ones around us.

Sometimes, we just need a change of scenery. Sometimes the memories we have that linger around us are situational or environmental. Getting out of town, moving, changing jobs, might be scary for some, but for others it may be a breath of fresh air, which is what we all need every once in a while. Fear of change is common, but that doesn't mean change shouldn't happen. I was deathly afraid of joining the military. I wasn't sure what was going to happen. We were at the tail end of a war, and people were still being deployed. I could've been one of them. The truth is, I turned my back to the edge of a cliff, put my arms out and leaned back; I asked a higher being to finally catch me and steer my life, because I just wasn't doing it right. I was tired of taking corners and going down dark roads to find a dead end only to turn around and come to another dead end. I needed direction, light, and hope. Not a sense of false hope. Yes, the military did this for me. No, it will not do it for everyone. Find your light, direction and hope. I'm not an advocate for joining the armed forces or joining The Peace Corp or for recreational drugs. I'm simply someone who at one-point thought about what they truly needed...what they TRULY wanted and made a big decision that they knew would change and impact their life for the better. You are certainly not alone. Remember, 1 out of 4. There's always a person to speak to about it. It doesn't have to be someone you know; they just have to support all of the above. You don't have to be religious or spiritual or anything (although sometimes belief systems really help a great deal) you just have to find a way to believe in your one true self. She/he is in there somewhere. One last task...

Sit in silence for a few minutes. Close your eyes. Remember the best times you can think of when you were a kid. What were you doing? Dancing? Skating? Chasing your brothers and sisters? Running through a field? Catching fireflies? Whatever it was, also try to remember your favorite pop/rock band. Try to remember that music you no longer listen to and go ahead and play it somehow. Find the music and blast it while remembering all those great times. Remember the movies that were your absolute favorite that

you could watch over and over again. Watch them. Right now. Those are your "go-to's." Those are your substances. Your brain is craving the release of endorphins, oxytocin, serotonin, and dopamine so desperately, but not the temporary/artificial kind; it's craving the long-term, child-like, care-free kind. The kind that last forever. Once you get good at producing them, your brain will remember how to make them on its own, again. Right now, it just needs a little help. If the pain you suffered requires professional help, get it. Free therapy is everywhere. Deal with all the struggles and finally release the pressure and weight that's been holding you down.

Muhammad Ali was an exceptional boxer for a living. He fought tirelessly, winning championships, yelling from the top of the mountains, "I am the greatest!" You too, are a fighter. You have your battles to fight every single day. Fight them and win! Even if you take a few hits, get back up and make a name for yourself. Just when you think it's time to give up, get back in the ring. The fights get easier and become less frequent when we train hard. Pretty soon you'll attract the right people around you. Pretty soon you'll be able to weed out the negativity in your life. Pretty soon the world around you will know your name. Pretty soon, you TOO, will be a champion!

PLEASE READ!!!

***This passage is in no way an official medical guide or guaranteed way to improve depression and anxiety. This is what worked for me. The guidelines are healthy and structured enough for me to put in black and white. I AM a success story of these methods, and I believe everyone can be a success story. If my methods do not work, seek other success stories with different methods customized for your lifestyle. It's important that you take charge of yourself and enjoy the life around you in a more care-free manner and spread the wealth of positivity. Although I still face struggles, I feel powerful and in charge. I no longer drown in my own despair or try to fulfill a void in unhealthy ways. I see clearer surroundings and manage to put actual future plans for my life in motion, without holding back. If I can do it, anyone can!*

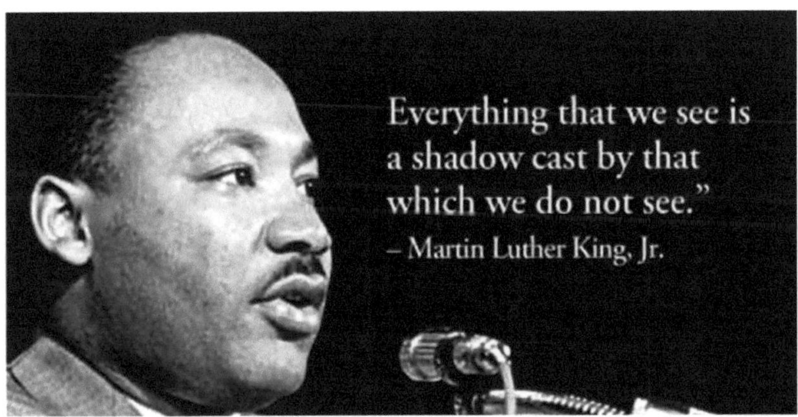

Hi! My name is Jenni. All my life I've worked on this writing thing…not because I want to be a writer or anything. Making a career out of something like this, for me, is like any person making a career out of converting oxygen into carbon dioxide. It's a part of me. I write things like fiction and the non-fiction and also poetry. I don't stick to any particular form of writing, although I don't always write how I speak; I write how I think. Ever put yourself in a situation where you really truly wish you could've said the very thing you thought of later on, in an argument, because it would've been an awesome comeback? It's why I lack a lot of social skills and am very awkward in a group setting. All my thoughts stay warm and cozy in my mind even when I want to say things, I don't. My thoughts throw down in writing, but not so much when I speak. I like to observe. Nothing wrong with being social, but in my opinion, when you're social, you're distracted; distracted from the very core of what makes you tick, what makes you sad, or what makes you happy, even. Being social doesn't always allow you to get to know yourself. That is why in this book I suggest dating yourself and getting to know yourself, that way you're not perfect strangers when reality hits every now and then, and so your head isn't such a dark place to be in.

Back to writing. I write fun things, real things, unreal things, and things that may or may not anger you. A lot of it is opinionated and based off my own experiences. I'm in no

way a licensed psychiatrist or doctor of any kind, but I do
(at times) have a pretty leveled head enough to give some
sound advice. You are the company you keep. If it wasn't for
some family and my amazing siblings, my beautiful wife, her
family, or the friends I grew up with, I wouldn't have gotten
through much of what I did. That's not to say I don't fully
understand someone who hasn't had such fortune, because I
do, to an extent. I know, that regardless of what happens in
your life, you're responsible for the end results…and that's
scary! What if something so terrible happens to you and
you're traumatized; no coming back from it? I'm here to say,
I've faced individuals (personally) who have had quite the
traumatic experiences; from deaths, to shootings to rapes,
homeless situations, addicts…and I'm here to say, I've never
seen so many comebacks in my life. Not all human beings
seem to exhibit the strength these individuals do, but ALL
are capable. The life inflicted upon you does not define you,
but your choices that follow sure do. No matter how down
you are, this is not your ending!

Being born in the *80s* and growing up in the *90s* is one thing...passion.
We grew up different than the ones before and after. Music was passionate and lyrics were deep.
A clothing drawer of *colors* and where standing out meant fitting in. Serotonin was high and the drugs were low.
Kids threw parties when their parents were out of town and it was always a night to remember.
Technology was new, rather than standard.
The generation where creativity meets intelligence.
The generation of skating rinks on the weekends and baggy pants and skater shoes even if you didn't skate.
Kids begged for their license and their necks didn't hurt from staring down.
♫ Songs were created, not digitally engineered.
Happy endings to movies that moved us and filled us with hope.
We're the generation that can watch our favorite Disney movies over and over and never get tired of them.

We handle our anxiety and depression with the outdoors and the good in life instead of drinking our life away and popping pills.
We have that extra spark in our souls that tells us to drive on when things get tough.
We "ran away" from home when we were upset with our parents then came back the same day.
We came from a place where having friends meant shoulders to lean on, positive affirmations, ride or die...the type of friends to go to breakfast on a Sunday to the local diner.
We're the 'sleepovers on weekends' generation, when good company outweighed the use of any cell phone.

The generation where we rang doorbells and surprised our family and friends with good company.

Why do kids these days feel anxiety and depression harder than most? Why does ringing a doorbell scare us? It's simple. Things went backwards.
More drugs were invented, more guns were possessed, more technology advanced, personal contact diminished to a breakup text.
⏱ Our lives are so over-scheduled and driven by pure stress. We have too many "knowns" now, that the *unknown* became scary. Instead of weathering the storm, the tough times reap entitlement, unhealthy coping, and broken souls because all of life's meaning has been reduced to a few narrowing factors: social media and politics.
If we had all grown up facing the world itself instead of a screen, we'd be in much better shape. If this generation raises their kids as their grandparents raised theirs, we can revert to a wiser, kinder, hardworking and stronger human race, knowing now, what we didn't know before.

Free therapy IS available!

Your Life Your Voice: http://www.yourlifeyourvoice.org/
(Phone, email and chat all available)

Center for Interactive Mental Health Solutions:
https://cimhs.com/

National Suicide Prevention Hotline: 1-800-273-8255

Military Crisis Line: 1-800-273-8255 (Press 1)

There are closed Facebook support groups available to
join as well.
You can maintain a safe space from your own home,
and still discuss concerns with those experiencing the
same mentality as you.
Just remember to be safe and discreet about your
identity!
In some groups, you may even remain anonymous.

Dedicated to my grandmother, Carmen. I love you!

Photos and illustration by Jenni L. Medina

Icon illustrations by Microsoft Word

Available on Kindle

© JUNE 27, 2019

www.ingramcontent.com/pod-product-compliance
Lightning Source LLC
Chambersburg PA
CBHW040317240726
48664CB00006B/1529